writing guides

ACTIVITIES FOR WRITING

Reports

HUW THOMAS

PHOTOCOPIABLE PHOTOC

NON-FICTION FOR AGES

5-7

CONTENTS

INTRODUCTION

The Scholastic *Writing Guides* series provides teachers with ideas and projects that promote a range of writing, bringing insights from educational research into the classroom. Each guide explores a different type of writing and provides example material, background information, photocopiable activities and teaching suggestions. Their aim is to enable teachers to guide the writing process, share planning ideas and develop themes as a context for writing activities.

The materials:
- motivate children with interesting activities
- break complex types of writing into manageable teaching units
- focus on and develop the typical features of particular types of writing
- provide original approaches to teaching.

Each book is divided into sections, beginning with examples of the type of writing being taught. These are followed by ideas for developing writing and projects that will extend over a series of sessions.

SECTION ONE: USING GOOD EXAMPLES

Section One looks at good examples of the genre, with the emphasis on using texts to stimulate and develop writing. Two example texts are shared, and questions that focus the discussion on their significant features are suggested. This is followed by activities that explore what the texts can teach us about writing, enabling teachers to compare the two texts and to go on to model the type of writing presented in the guide.

SECTION TWO: DEVELOPING WRITING

Section Two moves from reading to writing. This section provides activities that prompt and support children in planning and writing. A range of approaches includes planning templates and strategies to stimulate ideas. The activities refine children's ideas about the type of writing being developed and give them focused writing practice in the context of scaffolded tasks. Teacher's notes support each activity by explaining the objective and giving guidance on delivery.

SECTION THREE: WRITING

Section Three moves on to writing projects. Building upon the earlier work in Section Two, these projects aim to develop the quality of writing and provide a selection of ideas for class or group work on a particular theme or idea. The teacher may choose to use some or all of the ideas presented in each project as a way of weaving the strategies developed in Section Two into a more complex and extended writing task.

SECTION FOUR: REVIEW

Section Four supports the assessment process. Children are encouraged to reflect on the type of writing they are tackling and to evaluate how effectively their work has met the criteria for the genre identified in Section One.

Snails

by Nadia Rafia

Snails are small animals. They live in the garden. Snails usually live in dark places, like under stones or in old flower pots.

A snail has a hard shell that is usually brown and white, and a soft body. The soft body is called a foot. If a snail moves across glass and you look underneath it, you can see little lines moving down the foot. Snails move slowly. The snail's shell can grow. Every time it grows it adds another stripe to its pattern.

At the end of the foot there are two pairs of tentacles. A snail uses a lower pair for touching and smelling. The upper tentacles have got two eyes at the end. They also have a mouth.

A snail likes to eat fresh leaves and tomatoes. Its droppings are usually the same colour as its food. If it eats green food, its droppings are green. If it eats tomatoes, its droppings are red.

It can be relaxing to watch a snail.

Springwood

The School

Springwood is one of Sheffield's historic schools, built by the Sheffield School Board in 1875. Currently the school has pupils aged between 3 and 11 years. It has a 26-place Nursery for children under school age. There are 210 children at the school. The school is lively and interesting – with the children speaking 18 different languages.

The school provides good quality teaching in a calm, working environment. The school aims to maintain good relationships with the local community, respecting one another and working together.

"Pupils love coming to school and enjoy their learning."
Springwood OFSTED Inspection Report

SECTION ONE

USING GOOD EXAMPLES

In Section One, children are presented with two report texts. One is a child's piece of writing from the end of Year 2, the other is an extract from a school booklet written for parents.

Both these texts present the key features of report writing. They fulfil the purpose of stating what something is like or how things are. One is about a general subject, snails being quite common animals. The other focuses on a specific place. In both texts the writer is trying to enable the reader to see the subject clearly. The texts open with general statements and then qualify these statements with more detail.

The texts are written in the simple present tense. It is sometimes helpful to think of a report text as being like a photograph in words.

Shared activities

Snails

The text on photocopiable page 4 is an example to children of where their writing should be heading. It is a child's report text giving information gathered after a period of observing snails in a tank and making notes.

When reading this text with children, it would be useful to explore the way in which each paragraph develops separate pieces of information. Each paragraph has a different focus, such as food or habitat.

The text has numerous facts and it might be worth transferring the information into a list format, asking the children to list all the facts about snails that are presented in the text. You could challenge them to make the longest possible list.

Springwood

As children read the text on photocopiable page 5 they might want to think about how it would read if it had been written about their own school. The text gives a background to the subject, some details about the current numbers in the school and one interesting and unique fact about the place – the language diversity in the school. The second paragraph is less factual and centres more on what the school is like. The children could use this as a basis for devising sentences about their own school. These could be classed as paragraph A sentences (facts) or paragraph B sentences (opinions).

"Snails" notes

Planning notes are the basis of good report writing. On photocopiable page 8 we are given the notes that Nadia used to produce her report text about snails.

Begin by giving the children a copy of the notes, without displaying the text on photocopiable page 4. Ask the children to pick out facts about snails and to try to say these aloud as full sentences. After they have created a few such sentences, you can show them Nadia's text. They will start to see similarities between the notes and the text, and this is the point at which you can show how condensed the information is in the notes.

Ask the children to circle in the notes the facts that are disclosed in the sentences in Nadia's text – writers don't use every note they make in their final piece of writing.

Use the text

The text about Springwood School on photocopiable page 5, like any report, aims to communicate information. The activity on photocopiable page 9 involves the children in the process of retrieving information from the text. The seven quiz questions

writing guides: REPORTS

prompt them to look through the text for answers. Once they have tried this with the 'Springwood' text, they could try devising questions to use with the 'Snails' text.

Taking ideas further

Having explored two report texts, the following activities help the children to focus on elements that are appropriate for developing their report writing at Key Stage 1.

Report jumble

Children should begin the task on photocopiable page 10 by reading the texts that have been muddled up. Discourage them from saying aloud how they think the texts should join together because the next stage of this activity is for the children to cut out the strips and rebuild the report sentences. One of the vital elements of a report text is the way in which sentences qualify and develop subject matter. This will be developed more in Section Two. In this task children simply need to connect together the correct information sentences.

Report texts

Photocopiable page 11 offers some vital pointers for Key Stage 1 children beginning to engage in report writing. The introduction of a subject followed by the provision of details is essential to the structure of report texts. (This is particularly evident in the structure of the 'Snails' text on photocopiable page 4.) The use of the present tense and the connecting together of facts are other important elements; these are explored in the 'Report jumble' activity above, in which present-tense sentences unfold the information.

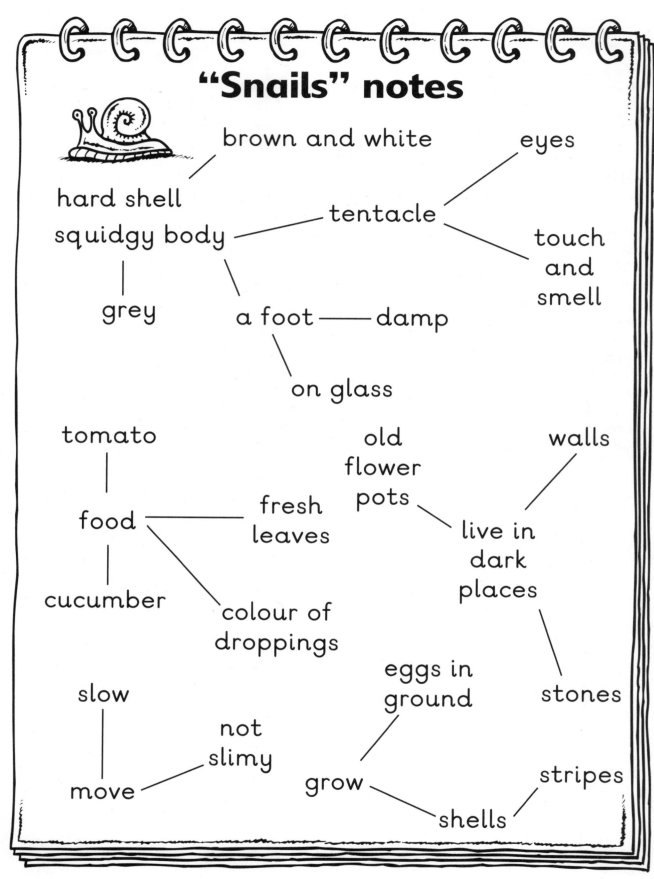

"Snails" notes

brown and white

eyes

hard shell

tentacle

touch and smell

squidgy body

grey

a foot —— damp

on glass

tomato

old flower pots

walls

food

fresh leaves

live in dark places

cucumber

colour of droppings

eggs in ground

stones

slow

not slimy

move

grow

shells

stripes

Here are Nadia's notes for her snail report. Circle things in her notes that you can find in her writing.

writing guides: REPORTS

Use the text

Can you use the text to answer these questions about Springwood School?

Where is Springwood?

How old are the pupils?

When was it built?

How many places are there in the Nursery?

How many children are there in the school?

What do the children think of the school?

How many languages are there in the school?

Report jumble

Here are some facts from the two report texts. They are split up and mixed up. Can you cut them out and put them back together?

The school is

Springwood is

two pairs of tentacles.

Snails are

The soft body is

small animals.

lively and interesting.

pupils aged between 3 and 11 years.

Currently the school has

a hard shell.

It has

one of Sheffield's historic schools.

At the end of the foot there are

a 26-place Nursery.

A snail has

called a foot.

writing guides: REPORTS

Report texts

Introduce a subject → Snails are small animals…

Give some details → It has a 26-place Nursery…

…children speaking 18 different languages.

Use present tense → The soft body is called a foot…

Snails move slowly…

Connect things up → At the end of the foot there are two pairs of tentacles…

The upper tentacles have…

SECTION TWO

DEVELOPING WRITING

In Section Two, children are taught skills that build towards good report writing. It includes activities that look at the features of report texts, allowing children to consider specific elements that can be reported on as well as the sentence structures used in such texts. A number of the activities can generate the writing of a short report, stemming from the tasks that the children have undertaken.

OBJECTIVE
■ To begin to make class notes for report writing.

IT INTERESTS ME

WHAT YOU NEED

Items that the children have brought in to school, board or flip chart, paper, writing materials.

WHAT TO DO

Ask the children to bring in to school something that interests them. It could be a toy or family photograph, a favourite cuddly toy, an interestingly shaped branch or shell – anything. Use these objects to stimulate a range of initial activities that will develop report-type sentences. For example, children:

● sit in a circle, and everyone tells the rest of the group what their interesting object is and says one thing about it (for example, *This is a photo of a dog*)

● each look at someone else's object and think of two sentences to say about it

● find similarities between objects (*These two are both red; These are both clockwork* and so on)

● list words about the object, including the name of the object, nouns for parts of it and adjectives describing it.

Use activities like these to create the stimulus for shared-writing activities in which you scribe some of the report sentences devised by the class. Allow this to lead on to children writing their own short reports about some of the objects discussed.

OBJECTIVE
■ To identify characteristics that will be discussed in a report.

THINGS TO SAY

WHAT YOU NEED

A range of objects (such as old wooden toys, kitchen utensils and so on), board or flip chart, paper, writing materials (including different-coloured marker pens).

WHAT TO DO

Display the objects and ask a child to select one of them. Tell the class that you are going to try to say everything you can about the object: what it looks like – its shape and colour, whether it has different parts joined together, and so on. Give a brief description of the physical nature of the object to the rest of the class and make some simple notes on the board.

Now focus on a different object and gather a range of comments about it from the children, noting these on the board. Repeat the process with several other objects.

Once this is done, look at the list of comments you have collected and, using different-coloured marker pens, circle similar comments. If, for example, the colour of the object has elicited comments, circle these in one colour. If different moving parts have been commented on, circle those in another. Try to identify the features that have been grouped together and write them on the board (for example, *parts of the object, size of the object*).

writing guides: **REPORTS**

Ask the children to choose an object from the collection on display and select one or two of these features as the basis for report sentences about the object, for example *There are moving parts in the whisk; The bat is very smooth.*

Now ask them to write a short report about their object, incorporating sentences adapted from the comments gathered by the class for other objects.

PICK IT APART
WHAT YOU NEED
Photocopiable page 17, paper, writing materials.

WHAT TO DO
Report writing relies upon the ability to recognise different characteristics of a subject and catalogue them for inclusion in a text. Ask each child to think of a subject about which they could write, steering them away from the subject matter of earlier reports. They could think of a place, such as their bedroom, or a favourite animal. If they have a favourite object, the weirder the better as they will find more to write about! Ask them to write down the title of their subject in the middle box of photocopiable page 17.

Encourage the children to think of ten different things they could say about their subject (for example, if it is their bedroom, *It has two windows; a matching rug and blind; a teddy on my bed*; if it is an animal, *It has a beak; pointed ears; a yellow head…*) and record them in note form, filling in each of the ten boxes on the photocopiable sheet. Once they have completed as many as they can, they should write their score in the space provided.

As a further activity, the children could use the notes they have made on the photocopiable sheet to write sentences about their subject. Ask them to think carefully about which fact to put first.

SUPERHEROIC REPORTING
WHAT YOU NEED
Any available merchandising from a current television programme or film (or the latest craze), board or flip chart, paper, writing materials.

WHAT TO DO
In the past I have done this activity with Transformers, Mutant Turtles and Pokémon. Who knows what shape it may take in the future! The idea is to undertake a shared session that constructs a report paragraph using a set of characters from a current television programme/film or craze that is generating a lot of enthusiasm. Ask the class in a shared session to think of a creature who has a starring role or special characteristics that would make it interesting as the subject of a report. For some reason this activity works best if the creature doesn't have a human form and features. Ask the children to list different things about the character, for example *got a spiral on its belly; fur which is red and soft; has a green beard; speaks in a strange language…*

Once four or five features have been listed, ask the children how they would turn the facts into sentences. Which fact would they put first? How would they turn it into a full sentence? Work through each feature, turning it into a report sentence.

When the children have completed a paragraph on one character, they can try it with another, possibly in a later session or as a homework task. These paragraphs will then form a simple report text, providing snapshot views of a current craze.

OBJECTIVE
■ To draft notes that could be used to write a report text.

OBJECTIVE
■ To write a simple report text, basing it on the subject's key characteristics.

OBJECTIVE
■ To develop detailed observation in report writing.

TREE SPLITS
WHAT YOU NEED
Photocopiable page 18, interesting subject matter, paper, writing materials.

WHAT TO DO
Ask the children to begin with a subject (it could be a museum artefact, a place or a toy, for example), record it in the far left box of photocopiable page 18 and think of three distinct features of the subject. If, for example, they are writing about the park they may write *the park* on the left and, in the three spaces leading from it, record *swings; climbing frame; lots of trees*. Having done this, explain that they should write briefly about each of the three features they have listed, If, for example, one of the features of the park is *climbing frame*, a child could write about the shape and height of the climbing frame, how new it is, what you can do on it, and so on.

Follow this activity with the children using their 'Tree splits' to write a short report about their subject, moving from general sentences (for example, *There are lots of things to play on in our park*) to more specific ones (for example, *The slide is very tall*).

OBJECTIVE
■ To organise information that is to be presented in a report.

ABOUT ME
WHAT YOU NEED
Photocopiable page 19, scissors, paper, writing materials.

WHAT TO DO
Photocopiable page 19 contains a selection of categories in which the children can record facts about themselves. Ask them to fill in each of the sections, cut them out and organise the facts into an order that they think would be appropriate in a report text about themselves. They might want to begin with a paragraph on their appearance, followed by facts such as their name and age, before moving on to the things they like. If they wish, they can discard a few categories, narrowing their focus to a smaller number of facts, or group different categories together. They may wish to give reasons for their preferences.

The completed categories now form a planning sheet from which the children can produce a piece of report writing about themselves.

OBJECTIVE
■ To develop children's use of the present tense in report writing.

IS, ARE, HAS, HAVE
WHAT YOU NEED
Photocopiable page 20, scissors.

WHAT TO DO
Report writing relies on the use of the present tense, giving a picture in words of what something is like or how things are. Photocopiable page 20 contains simple sentences for children to reconstruct, using the present tense of the verbs *be* and *have*.

Ask the children to cut out the words and phrases on the photocopiable sheet and experiment with making different sentences, for example *My friends are playing with me* or *My friends are good fun at school*. There is more than one way in which all the sections can knit together to create four sentences that make sense as well as retaining grammatical consistency. An important part of this task is children getting their attempts wrong and realising that the sentences created do not sound right. Saying them aloud is a vital step in distinguishing sentences that do or don't work.

KIM'S GAME

WHAT YOU NEED

A tray of 15 small items, as used in 'Kim's game', board or flip chart, writing materials, photocopiable page 18 (optional).

WHAT TO DO

'Kim's game' is the old party game in which 15 objects are shown to a group of children who then have to remember what they saw on the tray. In this version the tray is shown to the children for 15 seconds. The objects are then covered with a sheet and children have to recall what is on the tray. They also have to remember any facts about the objects, giving as much detail as they can, so instead of just saying *a dog* they can say *a brown, plastic dog*.

Use this activity to move on to a shared production of a written list of objects seen on the tray, with defining details.

Kim's game can be combined with the use of 'Tree splits' branches (see the activity on the opposite page). As with the original game, children look at the tray before it is covered. They then use photocopiable page 18 to guide them into the production of simple present-tense sentences about the objects they saw on the tray.

OBJECTIVE
■ To define features of an object.

SUBJECT CARDS

WHAT YOU NEED

Photocopiable page 21, scissors, paper, writing materials.

WHAT TO DO

Ask the children to cut out the subject cards on photocopiable page 21 and place them face downwards on the table. Explain that they should select a card, turn it face upwards and make some notes about that subject on a piece of paper. These may be short phrases or words, as in the 'Snails' notes (see photocopiable page 8), but they should have the makings of a report text. Once they have done this, explain that they need to imagine they are going to use their notes to write a report about the subject – but how would they start the writing? Remind them of the point made on photocopiable page 11 about starting with an introduction and developing detail; they also need to write in the present tense (see 'Is, are, has, have' above).

Ask them to write their opening sentences in full, then select another card, to begin the process again.

OBJECTIVE
■ To use the present tense and to move from general to specific information in report writing.

ABOUT US

WHAT YOU NEED

Copies of report texts generated in 'About me' (see the activity on the opposite page), paper, writing materials.

WHAT TO DO

Divide the class into groups of four to six. Ask each group to read all the reports for the children in their group. Explain that they then have to write a report sentence or paragraph about their group, focusing on one or two facts that they have found. This could be something as simple as the different eye colours in the group (for example, *Two of the group have blue eyes and four have brown eyes*), or it could be a statement that presents a brief summary, such as *Everyone in the group is the same age, but we all have different favourite foods*.

OBJECTIVE
■ To gather information from different sources for a report.

writing guides: **REPORTS**

OBJECTIVE

■ To understand that sentences can have different levels of detail in them.

SAME BUT MORE

WHAT YOU NEED

Photocopiable page 22, scissors, items from the 'Kim's game' tray (see the activity on the previous page).

WHAT TO DO

Begin by explaining the idea of sentences varying in how much detail they present to the reader. Use items from the 'Kim's game' tray to reinforce how a simple phrase can have detail added to it, reminding the children of the difference between *a dog* and *a brown, plastic dog*.

Now ask the children to cut out the sentences on photocopiable page 22 and, as a first step, to put sentences about the same thing into pairs. Once they have done this, they can decide which sentence in each pairing gives the greater detail. Let this lead on to a discussion about what has been added in the more detailed sentence.

OBJECTIVE

■ To use adjectives to provide more detail about a subject.

ADJECTIVES GAME

WHAT YOU NEED

Objects that lend themselves to interesting descriptions.

WHAT TO DO

Ask the children to sit in a circle. Explain how to play the 'Adjectives game': an object is passed around and the children take turns to think of a word that describes it, each child adding an adjective. If the object is a jumper, for example, the first child might begin with *a red jumper*. The next child might add the word *floppy*, making the phrase *a floppy, red jumper*; the next might add the word *old* – *an old, floppy, red jumper*. As it gets harder, allow other children to make suggestions to any children who are struggling to think of a word. Once they have exhausted the subject matter, move on to a different object to continue the game.

After the game, discuss the idea that a sentence doesn't have to be a simple statement such as *The jumper is red*; a sentence can say two things (or more!), using conjunctions – *The jumper is red and scruffy*. Compile a class list of interesting adjectives and ask the children to use them to write three sentences, each one stating something about one of the objects.

OBJECTIVE

■ To include greater levels of detail in report writing.

ADD DETAIL

WHAT YOU NEED

Strips of card, scissors, writing materials.

WHAT TO DO

Ask the children to write a simple report sentence on a strip of card, for example *The classroom has got a door*. Working with a partner, they should look for a place in their sentence where more detail could be added, and cut the strip in the place they have identified. For example, between the words *a* and *door* they could insert a colour word, to make *The classroom has got a blue door*. Other details can be added, by writing on separate strips of card, until they have a sentence with much more detail, such as *The Reception classroom has got a wooden, blue door with a window in it*.

writing guides: REPORTS

Pick it apart

Think of something you could write about. Then try listing ten different things you could say about that subject.

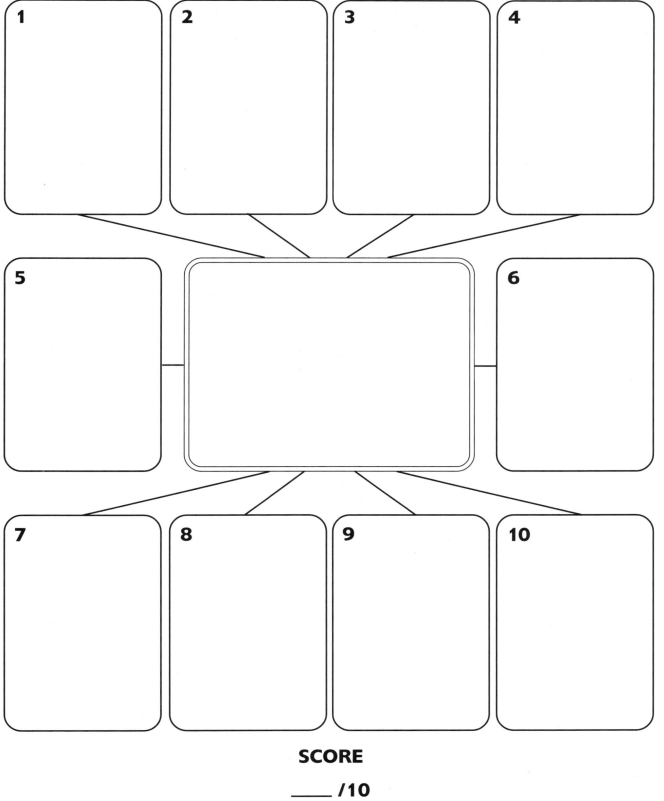

SCORE

____ /10

Tree splits

Start with a subject. Think of three things you can say about it. Then can you say a bit more about each separate thing?

SCHOLASTIC PHOTOCOPIABLE

writing guides: **REPORTS**

About me

Write some facts about yourself on these cards.

My name	Colour of eyes	Height
Favourite activity	My age	Where I live
What I think about school	Favourite food	My best place to visit
Something I don't like	A person I like to be with	Favourite smell
Favourite colour	A picture of my face	When I grow up I want to be...

Is, are, has, have

Try rebuilding these sentences.

Summer

playing with me.

has

is

We

got new trainers.

are

Joe

after spring.

My friends

have

good fun at school.

Subject cards

Choose a card which will be the subject of your report writing.
You will need to make some notes first.

what you can see through the classroom window	your friend	a shop you visit a lot
the weather today	the street where you live	your classroom
a packed lunch	your family	the school playground
your home	your teacher	a park where you play

Same but more

Find sentences that are about the same thing.
Can you see which sentence gives more detail?

If you push the switch, the light will flash.	The teddy has a button nose which I have sewn on.
The weather is sunny, but it is starting to rain.	The weather is sunny.
When the green person lights up, it is safe to cross the road.	The playground is warm.
The sun has made the playground warm.	The teddy has a button nose.
The light will flash.	It is safe to cross the road.

writing guides: REPORTS

By this stage, children will have explored some of the key features of constructing a report text, maintaining the four key aspects on photocopiable page 11:

- *introduce a subject*
- *give some details*
- *use present tense*
- *connect things up.*

They will have involved themselves in thinking of details to present when reporting on a subject, moving from the general to the specific and using present-tense sentences.

In Section Three, these elements of report writing are developed through three different writing projects whose focus is two creatures of the children's choice; a simulated location; and the children's own locality.

Creatures

In this project children write a report text about two different creatures, commenting on the similarities and differences between them. Being able to write about more than one subject is a crucial skill that children need to learn. Obviously the more firsthand experience children can bring to the planning of such writing, the better, which is why minibeasts, or even pets, would be a good subject for this activity.

Photocopiable page 25 can be used by the children to make notes about each creature they have chosen. Prompt questions down the sides have been given to stimulate ideas. Remind the children that they should not be trying to produce full sentences when they are note-taking – in fact, this will hold them back – they may find that a list of important words is enough.

Similar/different

Photocopiable page 28 provides a framework for the children to draw the two creatures that are the subject of their report and to note down similarities and differences between them. They should refer back to their notes on photocopiable page 25.

Encourage the children to use this stimulus to write a report about their two creatures. Suggest that they start with the sentence: (Name of creature 1) *and* (Name of creature 2) *are both…* Their report should involve some basic paragraphing, with the first paragraph being devoted to creature 1 and the second paragraph to creature 2; comments about similarities and differences between the creatures should be included in the second paragraph.

Funland

The scene depicted on photocopiable pages 26–7 can be used to prompt report writing. What can the children see in the picture? Ask them to help you to make a list on a board or flip chart of the features that are shown. Explain that in their report it will be important that they do not leave anything out, as it will be used as an information guide for visitors.

As the children write about Funland, encourage them to provide their own facts about the various features. For example, they might want to include a paragraph about the go-kart track; they should remember to progress from a general statement about it to more specific details such as how the go-karts move, how long each ride is, how much it costs, and so on.

The information guide could be produced using an alternative method: mount an A3 copy of 'Funland' onto a large sheet of paper, placing it in the centre and leaving plenty of room around the sides; each child can take one or two attractions (for example, the bouncy castle and the donkey rides) or simple features (for example, the car park and the picnic area) and produce a report paragraph for each one, to be placed around the edge of the picture with a line pointing to the appropriate location.

Guide map

The guide map that the children produce on an enlarged copy of photocopiable page 29 folds into three sections to form a leaflet on the children's local area. They should begin by drawing a simple map of their locality (on the central area of the photocopiable sheet); younger children may find it easier to draw a picture of the area instead. There is a line for the children to write the name of the area under the heading *Guide map*.

They should then identify four places in the locality about which they could report and which they have shown on their hand-drawn map. For example, these could be a local park, a popular shop or a community centre. It could also be a favourite place to walk or a place of interest.

Once they have done this, they should make some notes about each place on a separate piece of rough paper. (Again, the 'Snails' notes on photocopiable page 8 can be used to remind the children of the brief nature of note-making.) They can then use these to write four report paragraphs in the decorative boxes around the guide map. One paragraph could begin, for example, *The park is in the village. There is a big climbing frame and some swings. There are also tables for a picnic…*

As in the previous activity, 'Funland', lines can be drawn from the report texts to the features (on the map) they are pointing out.

When the children have folded their leaflet as shown below, they can finish the activity by working on the front cover, writing the name of the area that the guide map shows and decorating the page with their own illustrations of the locality.

Creatures

Creature 2

What does it look like?

What does it eat?

Where does it live?

How does it feel?

Creature 1

How does it move?

What is it like?

What is it called?

What does it do?

Funland

cable car

ski slope

kiddie farm

fun

railway

donkey rides

bouncy castle

roundabout

stalls

coach park

Similar/different

| Creature 1 | Creature 2 |

Name _____   Name _____

Picture

Picture

Think of three similarities between these creatures.

1 _____

2 _____

3 _____

Think of three differences between these creatures.

1 _____

2 _____

3 _____

ld

Guide map

to _____

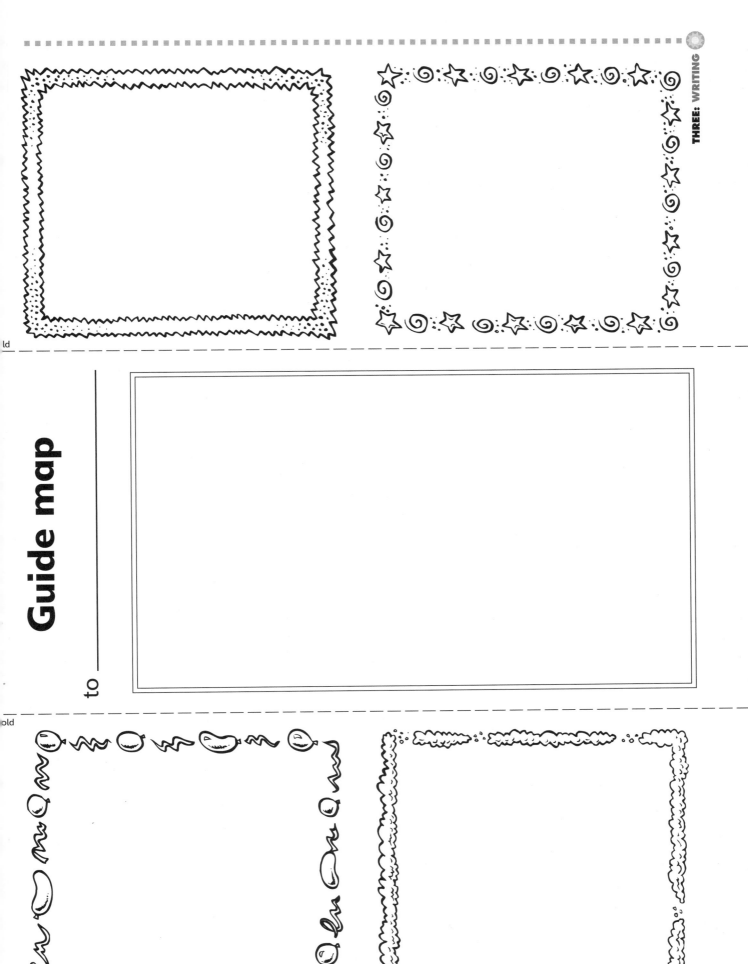

old

writing guides: REPORTS

SECTION FOUR
REVIEW

The two review photocopiable sheets in Section Four give the children the opportunity to evaluate their own writing of specific reports, and reports in general, with the aim of encouraging them to develop some ideas for future texts. The children can use the review sheets to look at the work they have done in Sections One, Two and Three.

Can you find…?

Photocopiable page 31 allows the children to draw on the skills they have learned in Sections One and Two. They need to look closely at their report text to find the features given on the photocopiable sheet and record examples. This will enable them to undertake an effective self-review of their writing. When reviewing reports, it is vital children see similarities in different texts they have produced. Sentences that are similar could include, for example, *My town is big* and *Funland is a big place*.

Questions answered

To complete photocopiable page 32 the children should look back at report texts they have created and find specific information that was presented in them. They should then think of three questions that would be answered by the facts they have given. For example, in the 'Snails' text (see photocopiable page 4) Nadia writes: *The soft body is called a foot*. So on photocopiable page 32 she could write the question *What does the snail's foot feel like?*

For the second part of the sheet, the children should think about what they might tackle in a future report. Space is provided for three questions that their report might answer.

writing guides: REPORTS

Can you find...?

Look at a report text you have written.
Find these things and write them here.

an opening sentence

_____

_____

a sentence that gives a detail

_____

_____

a sentence that uses present-tense verbs

_____

_____

a sentence that tells us more about something

_____

_____

two sentences that are similar

_____ | _____

_____ | _____

_____ | _____

_____ | _____

Questions answered

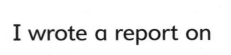

I wrote a report on

It answered these questions:

I could write a report on

and answer these questions:

writing guides: REPORTS